4-21-75

Teaching Creative Movement

The material contained in this book is applicable to all age groups from children through to adults. Its purpose is to serve as a guide for teachers who wish to introduce Creative Movement as a separate subject, as well as for those who would like to add another dimension to their own areas. It will be of value to students attending Teachers Colleges who plan to use Creative Movement in their work as educators and should also provide relevant in-service material for those already engaged in the teaching of Movement and Dance.

Creative Movement

Johanna Exiner
in collaboration with
Phyllis Lloyd

Photographs by Howard Birnstihl

Publishers PLAYS, INC. *Boston*

First American edition published by
PLAYS, INC. 1974

Library of Congress Cataloging in Publication Data
Exiner, Johanna.
  Teaching Creative Movement.

  Bibliography: p.
  1. Dancing-Children's dances. 2 Modern dance.
I. Lloyd, Phyllis, joint author. II. Title.
GV1799.E84 1975   793.3'2   74-14629
ISBN 0 8238 0177 2

Printed in Great Britain

Contents

Preface

In the course of discussing our diverse experiences in the field of Creative Movement and Dance, many ideas arose which we found were of interest and had possibilities for new development in teaching. Yet it was not until we were requested to devise a Curriculum Guide for pre-school children that we began to put our ideas down on paper. While working on this project, we found that the content areas which had to be covered within this particular framework were no different from those which were relevant to the teaching of Creative Movement to any age group. It was this fact which finally led us to undertake the writing of this book.

Although we had a different movement background, our common basis lay in the teachings of Rudolf Laban. In the process of clarifying our thoughts and ideas we found, however, that we needed to detach ourselves to some extent from his system and go our own way in our approach to the concepts and the practical application of Creative Movement. We hope that our readers will feel free to adopt a similar attitude and use the book as a source from which to develop their own ideas and to branch out into whatever direction their specific interests lie.

We wish to express our sincere appreciation to the Principal, Vice-Principal and the Staff of the Melbourne Kindergarten Teachers' College, who, all in their own way, contributed towards the gradual emergence of the thoughts which are contained in this book.

We are also very grateful to the Staff and children of the Powlett Reserve Kindergarten, to students from various schools and trainee-teachers from Melbourne Kindergarten Teachers' College and Mercer House for their co-operation. Much patient work was required by them to demonstrate effectively the different areas of Creative Movement represented in the illustrations.

Introduction

When looking at Dance throughout the ages, we find that, with certain exceptions, it has played a role in education since the beginning of mankind. In tribal societies, where no formal education existed, children learned from their elders all the skills necessary for adult living. Amongst these was dancing, which formed an integral part of the early life of man. Dances were performed on all occasions—birth, death, marriage, sickness, war, hunting and to honour and appease the gods and spirits. It was in this way that tribal man came to terms with his own feelings and with the inexplicable and often rather frightening happenings in the world around him.

In early civilisations, Dance became divided into various categories—some of a purely sacred nature, others for the celebration of festive occasions, and a new form which was designed for entertainment and especially arranged to please the eye. But there is evidence that dancing was also considered a way of learning, for as far back as the civilisations of Babylon and Ancient Egypt there are records of movement-pageants for the specific purpose of understanding the constellations and pathways of the stars.

In Crete, Dance was practised in a more systematic fashion in order to acquire physical skills and courage for warfare, and Cretan war dances, as well as many others, were later taken over by the Greeks who added variety and refinement to them. Eminent Greek philosophers expressed the opinion that Dance exerted a great influence on a balanced development of mind and body and advocated that it should be part of the education of all children, boys and girls alike. In Greece the Dance reached heights which so far seem to have been unsurpassed, particularly in the field of education. In a much broader sense educational value was also seen in the Greek theatre, which had its origin in ritual dances performed in honour of the god Dionysus and retained much Movement in its presentation.

Rome endeavoured to assimilate all facets of Greek culture, including the Dance, but was unable to absorb the spirit from which it had originated. Romans developed and excelled in the art of mime, but their dances soon became a purely erotic and often obscene form of entertainment. It was because of this that the early church forbade all forms of dancing, except for some movement patterns which were included in its rituals. The Dance could not become completely suppressed—it is too much ingrained in human nature—but it certainly reached an all time low during the early Middle Ages. It came to the fore in outbursts of dance-hysteria, as in the Dance of Death and the St Vitus Dance, and in contrast to these in the rather delightful dances of travelling entertainers. These lines of development did not occur in the countries of the East, where the Dance retained its initial role in the life of the community. The rise of the Renaissance in the Western world brought the Dance back into focus as a necessary part of education for young people of noble standing. It was considered to be one of the social graces they had to acquire and, to a lesser degree, a means of furthering their general development. Dances were very formal and their rules reflected the life-style of the society in which they were performed. This period also saw the Dance elevated to a highly respected but equally stylised stage-art.

Spontaneity survived in folk dancing, but when the growth of urban communities began to restrict or eliminate further development of village life the dances too became stagnant and were mostly performed for the sake of tradition.

In some of the early schools of the seventeenth and eighteenth centuries, stylised social dances were included as part of the curriculum and also many private dancing schools sprang up. Dancing of this formal nature was retained in education until, through the influence of Isadora Duncan, the importance of allowing children to express themselves freely through dancing was more clearly understood. Compared with our present ideas of creative freedom, Isadora Duncan's teaching was rather directive, yet it stood in contrast to the rigidity of the existing system. It appears that her approach was rather impulsive and lacked structure, therefore its validity for education failed to be fully recognised. It was not until Rudolf Laban established his methods of what he termed "Modern Educational Dance" that dancing gradually became a generally accepted facet of education in England as well as in other parts of Europe.

A similar development in the field of Dance in education took place in America, originating from the teachings of Gertrude Colby and specifically Margaret H'Doubler.

The urge towards expression through Movement seems to be inherent in man today as much as in the past, and its repression will have damaging effects on mind and body. Yet our social structure does not provide us with opportunities for expressing in Movement what we experience in our work and everyday life. Therefore opportunities have to be created to channel this vital and valuable drive in a way that makes it socially acceptable and gives it scope to contribute to the growth of the personality. Young children if given the opportunity will dance freely and naturally. As they grow older and become more exposed to the restricting influences of society, they often lose their ability to express themselves in Movement. Adults frequently find the experience of dancing strange and embarrassing, and any method of Movement Teaching should provide material both to liberate and to develop their movement potential. Suggestions guiding students to relate Movement to themselves and to their environment will have to be offered and group experience brought into focus which, if encouraged, will satisfy another need of the society in which we live.

We would like Dance to be once again a means of expression for the ordinary everyday person and not only for the talented few who make it their central interest in life. Everyone has some ability to express himself and be creative in Movement. If a student or group of students has found a new way of fulfilling a given task, we, as teachers, are satisfied that a creative process has taken place. We feel that we can disregard the fact that a similar solution may have been found before. The value of the creativity with which we are concerned lies in finding combinations in Movement which are personal and express individual ideas. Dance is the only form of creative expression which requires no other means than the body. To many students this in itself will give a sense of fulfilment, while others may find the experience valuable as an extension of their particular field of art or learning.

Over the years the word "Dance" has become associated with conventional as well as pre-arranged steps and often with formal presentations. It is for this reason that we have chosen to refer to our work as Creative Movement. This does not imply that it is less demanding or necessarily less artistic; the results will have content and genuine feeling even if they lack a high degree of precision.

Within the context of this book we use the term "Dance" to describe the work of a student or student group whose involvement with a particular theme takes them past the stage of being satisfied with movement experimentations. They will then take the step of selecting movements which they feel express most sensitively and clearly what they wish to "say", and of organising them into a coherent and distinctive pattern. There are no specific rules to be followed when working out such movement compositions. Each topic contains a number of latent structures, and students have to work towards discovering the one that will provide the right frame for the development of their idea. The solution which students arrive at through this process must stand up to their emotional and aesthetic demands and will be considered as final at that particular time.

Not everyone desires to give his movement studies such a degree of permanency, and attempts to do so may in fact destroy what has been spontaneously created. To those who are primarily concerned with Creative Movement as an experience, the fixing and retaining of movement patterns is of no special value. This applies almost without exception to young children and also to a good many adults. Improvisations can be considered as an alternative goal—their success depends less on the conscious process of organising and defining movement patterns and more on the ability students acquire to do this spontaneously while working on a particular theme. With an increase in skills and the application of a richer movement vocabulary, improvisations can in themselves become well rounded studies of high standard.

3

4

1 Content Areas of Creative Movement

The purpose of presenting all the content areas of Creative Movement in dial form is to establish, from the outset, that they should always be seen as one. Although each segment has to be worked on separately it should not be allowed to stay in isolation for any length of time. Students have to be aware of its place in the whole structure even while they are working on a single aspect. This requires specific practices to alternate with free experimentation on a wider scale, a fact which also ensures variety in programming. After a more general introduction, single areas can be developed in greater depth, which will lead to a fuller understanding of movement content and a greater clarity of expression. This process would be comparable to making a rough sketch of the whole structure of Movement and then gradually filling in the finer details.

In addition to giving a picture of Creative Movement as a whole, we suggest that the dial can also be used to analyse single movements. To illustrate this we have chosen as an example the simple gesture of Rising and Sinking, performed with the whole body by stretching up high and then lowering oneself to floor level.

A positive inner attitude for the movement will prevent it from becoming mechanical and will contribute towards its Fluency. Body Awareness will enhance the experience of every stage through which the movement proceeds and adequate skill will facilitate its performance. Awareness of Space (e.g., the shapes which the body assumes and of the pathways between them), the amount of Force used and the Time-quality with which it is dispensed, will give the movement form and dynamics. If the students are fully involved in the experience of Rising and Sinking this will in itself become a theme (from within "Movement" itself, see p. 36). Alternatively, it may become the

5

means of interpreting the movement of a fountain (from "The World Around" p. 38), or express joy or despair (from "The World Within" p. 40), and by doing so touch on other areas outside the actual field of Movement. This specific task (of rising and sinking), like all other tasks in a Creative Movement lesson, allows for individual interpretation within the given frame and this provides a link with the mover's personality. Relationships to partners or groups may not be specifically stressed, but as, within the context of this book, we look at Movement as a group activity, the awareness of others will in some way be present at all times.

It would stand to reason that neither teacher nor student should think of all these aspects while teaching or dancing, as this would turn a sensitive experience into an intellectual exercise. What in fact needs to take place on the part of the teacher is that, having assimilated all aspects of Movement to the extent that they are accessible to him without effort at all times, he can draw upon them whenever the need arises. In the process of teaching, all these facets of Movement will gradually be transmitted to the students, so that they in turn can absorb them. This is the goal to be attained, to a greater or lesser degree, by each student group, depending on their maturity level and the timespan available for teaching them.

There is, of course, the need to present and develop movement material in a systematic fashion. After giving the matter of priorities a great deal of thought, we decided that the awareness of the body and its movements should be given primary consideration, as these will provide the means for experiencing movement qualities and for the interpretation of feelings and ideas.

Key for Chapters 2, 3 and 4

We hope that the format chosen for the next three chapters will clarify the relationship between the concepts and the practical application of Creative Movement.

All pages on the left-hand side of these chapters are concerned with definitions and discussions of the various concepts of Movement. All pages on the right-hand side provide suggestions as to how these concepts can be experienced. We would expect teachers not to limit themselves to the practices we have recommended but together with their students find additional ways for further explorations. The movement ideas suggested in the succeeding three chapters do not constitute movement programmes in themselves but are meant to be used to provide material for parts of movement programmes.

For planning of complete programmes, see Chapter 5.

Touch and vision intensify kinesthetic experience

2 The Body

The body, because of its nature, is designed to be a sensitive receptor of impressions from "The World Around". In the society in which we live, few people sufficiently respect these physical attributes and tend to consider them merely as a means to fulfil the everyday functions of living. Children appear to be more in tune with their bodies and use them more fully in everything they do. Adults, who on the whole do not allow themselves a similar involvement, tend to miss out on many aesthetic experiences which can be transmitted to them through the senses. One of the aims of Creative Movement is to help students realise the connection physical perception has with feelings and intellectual awareness. A full integration of all these faculties is necessary to make the creative process complete.

Creative Movement relies on the body to a much greater extent than other areas of creativity. Movement sensations depend on the function of the kinesthetic sense: the sense of movement perception which provides the physiological basis for the experience and aesthetic appreciation of Movement. The senses of vision, touch and balance further contribute to movement awareness and so increase the satisfaction one can gain from all physical activities.

Presenting opportunities to develop these senses in the Creative Movement situation will help students become more confident in their creative abilities and will enable them to establish a more positive relationship towards their physical and emotional environment.

9

Contact with the floor increases the awareness of different body parts

(a) Body Awareness

Body Awareness is the basis for meaningful movement experience. We see it as comprising several factors:

a physical awareness of the body and limbs;

an understanding of their specific movement functions;

an appreciation of the body as a medium for creative expression.

In order to give Movement sensitive quality, Body Awareness must be accompanied by a corresponding inner awareness. This inner awareness or involvement of feeling will prevent Movement from becoming mechanical.

We believe that Body Awareness is best attained through moving, while other schools of thought, particularly of the East, advocate concentration on the body during stillness. In either case, the attention must be focused on the sensing of the body and not on the movements it might perform.

Body Awareness will lend confidence to the actions of everyday life by producing a sensitive physical presence and an easy orientation in Space. These same qualities will also contribute to the imaginative and versatile use of the body in the Creative Movement situation.

Some suggestions for experiencing Body Awareness:

These may consist of moving different body parts in isolation, e.g.,

head	grip it, nod, shake, roll it
neck	can experience twisting, craning, pulling in Recognition and awareness of different parts of the
face	can be effected through lifting *eyebrows*, wrinkling the *nose*, changing the shape of the *mouth*, fluttering the *eyelids*
hands	*fingertips*, *palms*, *knuckles*, *backs of hands* . . . can be brought into contact with each other or with the floor in different ways, gently touching or stroking, firmly clapping or gripping, clenching, spreading, wriggling
feet	can be manipulated in a similar manner and walked on in various ways
torso	awareness of different parts of the torso can best be felt by rolling on them, wriggling them, and "pointing" with them in various directions
knees	can bob up and down, shiver
shoulders	can shrug, wriggle, droop
elbows	can draw patterns on the floor or in the air, also "punch holes"
arms	can swing, circle
legs	can also swing and circle . . . and the weight can rest on different parts of them: side of the thigh, shin, etc
joints	can be explored for their mobility, viz., flexion, extension, abduction, adduction, rotating

Experiences have to be offered in which the student becomes aware of the fact that when several body parts move simultaneously, one or the other is leading the movement, e.g., in an upwards movement of the whole body the lead can be taken by head, hands, shoulder, feet, etc. Similarly, hands can "show the way" in walking or running, or shoulders and backs can be used to "push their way through space". Elbows can take the lead when turning. Placing the emphasis alternatively on different body parts makes the students feel them more intensively.

Any of the preceding suggestions can be developed into making *movement sequences:*

Wavelike rippling passing through the hands, arms, torso

Triggering off movements by contacting one body part with another, e.g., a hand tapping the opposite shoulder which in turn touches the knee, the knee taking the movement on to the forehead, etc

Movement studies (improvisations or dances) which may arise from experiences in Body Awareness may be Dance of Hands, Dance of Feet . . . "Smoothing" the Space Around, using the whole body

Alternatively, ideas can be introduced which will draw specifically on the experience of Body Awareness as material for interpretation, for example: Awakening, Dancing in the Wind, etc.

11

(b) Body Activities

When people dance they seem to make use of certain basic activities: locomotion, turning, elevation, falls and gesture. We believe that all movements of the body can be loosely grouped into these five sections. Body Activities form the natural vocabulary for Creative Movement expression.

The difference between the practices for Body Awareness and the exploration of Body Activities lies in the change of emphasis from the awareness of the body part itself to the movement it performs.

Each Body Activity can be explored in isolation as well as in different combinations. Some movements are more easily performed on their own while others need co-ordination between different body parts for fluent performance. We consider it best to let students discover for themselves how to co-ordinate movements, as superimposing rules from the outside may create tensions and so inhibit the students' natural flow of movement. Giving them scope to use their own movement combinations will gradually enable students to develop an original style.

Definition of Body Activities:

Locomotion: Travelling along the floor as in walking, creeping, crawling, etc.

Turning: Movements in which the body changes front.

Elevation: Taking off from the floor.

Falls: Movements which result in the major part of the body reaching floor level.

Gesture: Movements performed by the head, torso or limbs which do not necessarily involve any other Body Activity. (These can be done from a variety of stances, e.g., standing, sitting, kneeling, lying, etc.)

Some suggestions for experiencing Body Activities:

1. Locomotion

   Students can be encouraged to move along the floor with the weight placed on different body parts, e.g., sliding on backs, stomachs, walking on different parts of the feet, on the knees, buttocks, rolling, somersaulting, etc.

   With varying use of Movement elements very interesting results can be achieved.

   Sequences of Locomotion can be made by combining movements, e.g., a walk, a crawl, a slide on the back, a somersault, a roll, a slide on the stomach, etc.

2. Turning

   Turning can be explored along the same lines as Locomotion, e.g., on one or both feet, knees, buttocks, stomachs

   (Care must be taken not to expect students to sustain turning beyond what they feel is comfortable as it can lead to dizziness.)

   Sequences of Turning from feet to knees to buttocks; from one foot to the other, etc.

3. Elevation

   Students should be encouraged to experiment with the different ways of taking off from and landing on the floor, e.g., hopping, skipping and jumping. The latter can be varied as follows: from both feet to both feet, from one foot to both feet, from both feet to one foot, from one foot to the other foot as in hurdling. Skilful taking off for elevation will give greater height and/or distance and skilful landing will prevent jarring. Attention should be given to the weight of the body being pushed off from the ball to the toes of the foot and being caught in the reverse way, using the rest of the foot as a cushion.

   Elevation practices are difficult to sustain for young children and need to be introduced in combination with body shape in landing, arm gestures, turns and specifically with alterations of speed and rhythm. They rarely gain the experience of suspension which makes elevation so pleasurable for those who have acquired this skill.

   Sequences of Elevation: hopping on alternate legs; skips ending with a jump onto both feet; skipping interchanging with hurdling, etc.

4. Falls

   Falling can be experienced from various stances, e.g., kneeling, crouching, standing, etc., followed by landing on different body parts. It can be felt as a collapse or as an active downwards movement as in a "soft landing" or else throwing oneself on the ground. Falls can be varied further with regard to the body part leading the downward movement.

   Sequences of Falls: Interesting combinations can be achieved if falls from different stances and with different body parts leading are linked with

Skills

In the course of discussing Body Activities, we have to take into consideration the physical skills necessary to gain adequate control over body movements. The ability to move the body freely and skilfully will widen the range of creativity and enable the students to experience increased satisfaction from their efforts. The involvement with an idea and the desire to explore it more fully often develops skills incidentally. This sometimes makes students perform movements they would have thought to be outside their capabilities. The discovery of this process will give students confidence and make them more enterprising with regard to movement explorations. On the other hand, there are students who encounter a great deal of frustration through lack of technique. An observant teacher will in this case help a student to acquire the specific skill which is lacking or, if this is not possible, suggest other means of solving a particular task. This indirect teaching of skills can be an alternative to a more direct method which consists of routine exercises being practised regularly to be of benefit to all participants. The teacher who uses this method may also offer concrete suggestions for combining certain Body Activities in unusual ways in order to draw attention to movement sequences that students may not have discovered for themselves. This may appear to many as being too "teacher directed", while the disadvantage arising from the indirect method may be seen in the limitations which individuals or groups may set upon themselves. The choice between the two depends on the teacher's personal beliefs as well as the needs of the group. If a teacher can have students for a limited time only, such as in a school situation, it would appear that the indirect method is more appropriate in order to give priority to creative explorations.

various ways of rising, e.g., sidewards fall from knees—rise to feet—backwards fall—somersault landing on knees, etc.

5. Gesture

    Students need to explore the maximum range of movements which head, torso and limbs are able to perform, e.g., rotating, flexing, stretching, twisting, shaking, etc., of parts of the arm, such as fingers, wrists, hands, elbows, as well as movements of the whole arms. Gestures of the legs can be explored in a similar manner. Isolated gestures can be performed with parts of the torso, e.g., shoulders, hips, intercostals, etc. More complex torsal movements are body circles, body waves and other body gestures, e.g., curling, stretching, opening, closing, twisting. All gestures can be done purely as an exercise to discover and to extend the range of mobility. If related to other aspects of Movement their practice can lead to very interesting and imaginative movement patterns.

    Sequences of Gestures: Body parts can move towards and away from and around each other, in parallel and in opposite directions, alternately, simultaneously, etc. Any examples one might give for the limitless variety of these possibilities will tend to be arbitrary and much more original work can be done by individual experimentation.

Each Body Activity can in itself become the theme for creating improvisations and dances or else will be drawn upon when interpreting topics from "The World Around" and "The World Within".

> Gesture will feature more prominently in themes such as Vines and
>   Eastern Goddess;
> Locomotion in Hide-and-Seek and Hunted;
> Turning in Whirlwind and Confusion;
> Elevation in Jumping for Joy and Firecracker;
> Falling in Clowning and Exhaustion.

Suggestions for *grouping* of Body Activities taken from different sections may be as follows:

> crawl – rise – sink; run – jump – fall; walk – skip – turn; . . .

Fluent execution of such sequences depends largely on skilful transitions from one activity to the other. Making sequences repetitive helps to develop continuity and trains the mind to memorise Movement.

Body Activities represent the vocabulary of the dancer. Some students use them spontaneously and imaginatively, others need much encouragement. This can be provided by verbal suggestions while students are dancing, such as: "Could this make you feel like turning?", "Are you thinking of your arms?", "Perhaps you need to add a jump", etc. Such comments will open up new avenues for exploration and allow students to follow up whichever suggestion might appeal to them. By encouraging students to show to each other some of the new movements evolving from such practices, the movement vocabulary of the whole group can be enlarged.

15

(c) Relationships

The discussion in this section will centre around movement relationships which can be established between partners and groups. Any area of Movement can serve as a basis for such interactions; the personal attitude of group members to each other will often be reflected in the way in which their joint movement patterns evolve. Some students may have difficulties in "tuning in" with each other at first, yet by overcoming their initial reticence they enter into new and rewarding fields of movement experience. Establishing connections through using properties and percussion instruments often facilitates partner work, and the handling of such materials while engaged in Movement creates a variety of interesting sequences. For the very young it may be necessary to establish a focal point to which partners can relate themselves, or else restrict the area in which they are to move in order to prevent them from losing contact with each other. On the whole, group work with young children should be allowed to develop spontaneously. Special planning should be reserved for older groups.

Left: Relationship through movement
Right: Relationship through shape

Suggestions for establishing movement relationships between partners and groups:

Links between partners can be established in the more usual way by joining hands or leaning against each other's shoulders or backs, but students should also be encouraged to search for more original ideas. Emphasis on points of contact will bring into focus Body Awareness. Body Activities will provide the various ways for moving which can be done either:

alternately, leading to a kind of movement conversation;
simultaneously, which can be mirroring or copying each other; or
contrasting movements.

Large groups can work in *unison, canon* or *contrapuntal* forms. It is the spatial aspect of Movement which appears to be the governing principle in group work and this can be varied in the following manner:

Shapes of groups can change with regard to size, level and contour.
Pathways can change by moving towards, away, over, under and around each other as well as at varying distances.
Groups can form *circles* of variable size and height . . .
lines of varying length . . .
clusters of different contours and densities . . .

Practices can emphasise similarities as well as contrasts between the different shapes and pathways. All other aspects of Movement will play their usual role in further determining the dynamic qualities of these interactions.

Examples for making *movement sequences* with partners and groups:

Shapes can be extended and the pathways of one student can be continued by others.
One group can remain stationary while another moves and then changes activities.
Patterns can be broken up and re-formed.

The character of these sequences can be varied by changes in speed and rhythm, lightness, strength and the degree of Fluency applied.

Any aspect of partner work can become a theme for *movement studies:*

Leading and Following
Waxing and Waning
Dispersal and Gathering

Work *with one partner* will feature more prominently in topics such as:

Action and Reaction
Shadows
Friendship

Work *with groups* will feature in:

Kaleidoscope
Molecules
Clouds
Gang Warfare

Movement Dynamics and expression are apparent in play

Movement experiments in the playground

3 Principles of Movement

The basic principles governing Movement are generally recognised to be Force, Space and Time. Every movement can be accurately described by the amount of Force it contains, the pathway it follows in Space and the speed, rhythm and duration of its progress. In addition to these, all Movement contains a degree of Fluency which becomes evident in the free or hesitant manner in which a movement or movement sequence proceeds. Movement analysis, based on these principles, will make it possible to understand Movement better wherever it occurs. When considering movement responses of the human body, Force, Space, Time and Fluency must be seen as an integral part of every Body Activity. Students need to become familiar with all aspects of these elements of Movement through practices in Body Activities, so that later they may draw upon them when interpreting different movement themes.

Movements which students themselves create can obviously not be measured against any existing pattern, nor should they have to comply with the taste or style of a particular movement teacher. Their quality will depend primarily on the awareness of movement elements and the ability of the students to use them with sensitivity to give each movement form and Dynamics. Achievement can be assessed by the degree to which students are able to clarify and define their own movement patterns—where they go in Space, how forceful they are and at what speed or rhythm they wish them to be carried out. Disregarding the measuring of skills attained, we consider movement elements to be the only tangible criteria for evaluation inside the sphere of Creative Movement. Students' imagination needs encouragement and appreciation but would suffer if subjected to much criticism.

Using movement elements as guidelines makes it possible to teach students the structure of Movement and so provide them with the foundations on which they can build up their own movement ideas.

(a) Space

We see any Movement as forming a "design" in Space. Movements can go along straight or curved lines which in turn create angular or circular *air and floor patterns*. A pause in Movement will intensify the awareness of the *shape* which the body creates. It is important to realise that at every stage the whole body is involved in making these spatial patterns even while one or the other body part takes the lead. Clarity of form is as much dependent on Body Awareness as on an understanding of spatial relationships.

In our approach to Creative Movement students are encouraged to look at "Space" as a tangible material to work with and "Movement" as creating a discernible imprint upon it. This makes movement patterns appear less transient and thereby promotes in students a more responsible attitude towards clearly defining line and form.

All spatial design is developed by students themselves and should arise in the course of their experimentations with the theme they choose to interpret. This process allows for development of originality in single movements as well as for diversification in the spatial organisation of a composition.

Opening out

Suggestions for experiencing aspects of Space:

Body Activities can follow *straight lines* which will lead to *angular patterns*, e.g., zig-zags or symbols composed of straight lines as in the numbers 1, 4 . . . or the letters T, N, Z . . . as well as in figures like triangles and squares.

Body Activities along *curved lines* will result in *circular patterns*, e.g., wavelines, curved numbers, such as 6, 8, and letters S, C, O.

Straight and curved lines can be combined in 5, 2, G and J, for instance, or lead to many and varied abstract patterns.

The feeling evoked by the more *abrupt* changes of direction when creating angular patterns is very different from the more *fluid* transitions experienced when following a curved pathway, as is *increase* as against *decrease* of *size*. The characteristics of any pathway are further determined by the *direction* it takes into the different *areas* and *levels* in Space. Pathways can be seen as *radiating* from the body as well as *connecting* different outlying points with each other. Pathways can be *retraced* and this will increase the awareness of them.

21

During Movement, *body shape* will naturally blend with either the angular or curved patterns which are being created, but they will be felt more intensively in stillness. Shapes may involve the whole body or be formed by fingers, arms, legs . . . they can be symmetric, asymmetric, curled, stretched, twisted, narrow, wide, flat, voluminous, etc. They should not be seen as isolated poses, for any shape is the direct result of its preceding pathway. Shapes can be created on a variety of bases (they "feel" very different when using knees, the back, one or both feet, etc., as a platform), which can be held or changed while moving along, or while jumping, landing, turning and falling.

We have found that, on the whole, students are rather inhibited in their use of Space. Older students in particular find it difficult to make free use of floor space unless reminded of the possibilities that locomotion offers for varying movement patterns. All age groups also tend to forget about the additional "height" that can be gained by means of elevation and often restrict themselves to "filling in" the more immediate areas around their bodies with gestures. They need much encouragement to explore Space in all its aspects.

Sequence of shapes are interesting as well as comparatively simple practices. They may proceed from wide to narrow to tall . . . from curled to stretched to twisted . . . from large to small to medium . . .

The practice of changing shapes can be experienced as a *sequence of pathways* if the attention is focused on the movement which establishes links between them. Another way of introducing sequences of air and floor patterns is to suggest the formation of a series of numbers and letters and to experiment with different ways of arranging their positioning in Space. They can be made close together or far apart, they can lie in different planes and/or on different angles, they can be isolated, have points or lines of contact, or merge into each other. They can be "written" by means of gesture from a stable base and also while turning, in elevation and falls, or traced as a floor pattern by locomotion.

In addition, other well-known figures can be designed such as spirals. As already indicated it is important to keep in mind that not only gesture but all Body Activities can be experienced with emphasis on line and shape, e.g., circular or angular jumps, twisted falls, spiral turns. We think it advisable not to give any further specific examples as they may detract from the wide range of possibilities that can be explored.

Any aspect of Space can in itself become the theme for improvisations or dances, e.g., Circles, Angles. Spatial awareness will be more prominent in topics from "The World Around" and "The World Within", such as Caged, Lost in Space, Tangles.

Levels

23

From tension to buoyancy

(b) Force

It appears that Force gives to Movement a quality of "substance". *Strong* movements are usually felt as being solid and earthbound and easier to experience in a downward direction. *Lightness* on the other hand will create shapes and movements which tend to strive upwards and their experience will be one of suspension and buoyancy. *Heaviness* results from lack of muscular control and need not be connected with the actual weight of the body. Slightly built people can move strongly and heavily built people can move lightly; either will move heavily if they lack physical skills or have some inner resistance to using them adequately. Muscular control over the weight of the body will also make it possible to *transfer weight* with ease from one body part to another and obtain *balance* in a variety of positions.

A wider range of movement experience will be opened to students as they acquire the ability to vary all aspects of Force in a skilful and sensitive manner. Students should be given freedom to experiment with these, yet some direction may be advisable in the early stages as the appropriate use of Force contributes towards clarification of movement patterns.

Strength shadowed by lightness

25

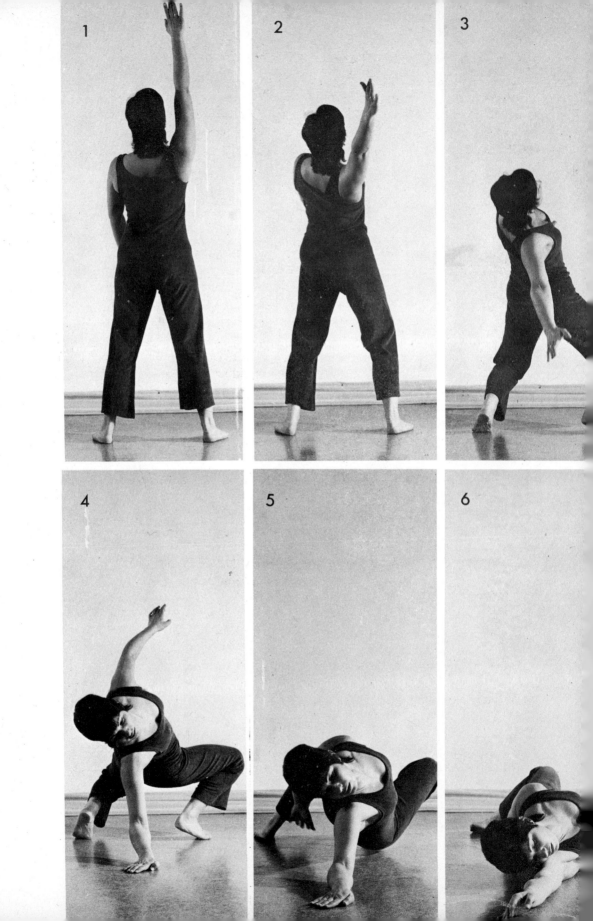

Suggestions for experiencing aspects of Force:

The feeling of Force in Movement will be attained by performing Body Activities in a *strong* or a *light* manner. The experience of strong movements can be stimulated by introducing movement words which describe strong actions, e.g., push, bump, break, hit, kick, trample, clench, struggle.

Lightness would be encouraged by movement words such as stroke, smooth, drift, sway, slither, evaporate.

The creative interpretation of such words will not be confined to the way these are normally performed. "Clenching", for instance, can be experienced as a contraction of various parts of the body, and "smoothing" can be done with the back, the side of the body, the head, etc.

Transference of weight can be experienced by changing the base on which the weight of the body is supported, for example, from the back to the feet, from one foot to the other. Many practices in weight transference will involve locomotion, but in this context it should not become the primary experience. The *sense of balance* plays an important part in all Movement. One can experiment with it by taking up a variety of body shapes over the same stable base; it comes into play when weight is transferred as well as in all Body Activities. *Off balance* actions are produced when the centre of gravity which has been established in a balanced position is shifted so far out that over-balance will result unless a compensatory move is made.

Refinement in the use of the Force element needs experience in moving with gradual and abrupt changes in the degree of intensity. These variations can occur in one Body Activity or within a group of Activities. *Heaviness* can be interpreted by not making use of the muscular energy necessary to control whatever movement may be performed. This will result in actions such as dragging, slouching, stumbling, etc. Or it may be expressed in the muscle-bound actions of wrestlers and weightlifters or in the rigidity of a robot.

Any of the preceding practices can be developed into making *sequences* of strong or light movements or into a combination of the two. Groups of Body Activities can contain:

> an increase or decrease of strength or other variables in intensity;
> weight transference which may include both balanced and off balance actions resulting in rather interesting combinations.

Any of these aspects of Force can in themselves become a theme for improvisations and dances, e.g., Lightness, Balance, or they can be drawn upon as a means for interpreting topics from "The World Around" or "The World Within".

> Strength will feature prominently in themes such as Power, Bouncer, etc.
> Lightness in Smoke, Gaiety;
> Weight transference in Acrobatics, Astronauts;
> Balance in Tightrope Walkers, Stability;
> Off balance in Toppletoy, Giddiness;
> Heaviness in Robots, Collapse.

27

ight transference

(c) Time

While Force gives Movement substance, and awareness of Space clarifies form, it is *rhythm* and *speed* which make Movement feel alive and vital. Students create their own rhythms and move at whatever speed the theme demands, but support in the form of sound accompaniment will provide additional ideas and inspiration for movement practices. With growing experience students will be able to combine rhythmic patterns into movement phrases and so learn a fundamental skill necessary for the organisation of movement studies.

Sound need not provide students with the rhythmical structure for their movement patterns; dancing without leaning on musical accompaniment is challenging and requires sensitivity to the rhythmical demands made by Movement itself. It allows for complete creative freedom and the development of an inner rhythmical discipline which is bound to be more meaningful than any which might be imposed from the outside.

Acceleration

Suggestions for experiencing aspects of Time:

Isolated or combined Body Activities should be performed at a quick or a slow pace, with acceleration or deceleration or sudden changes of tempo. Variations in *speed* can be further encouraged by introducing movement words such as hurried, racing, non-stop as against leisurely, languid, lazy; quicken, drive, urge on as against retard, check, throttle.

Sequences which focus particularly on the experience of speed should be introduced by making use of contrasting qualities, e.g., quick running, slow walking, stop. This will later lead to more refined grading, e.g., an accelerating run to a jump, a decelerating turn to a gradual stop.

Duration of either quick or slow movements can only be experienced between two moments of stillness. Awareness of duration will be increased if the Body Activity and its speed remain constant, e.g., a quick short run, pause, as against a quick long run, pause, etc. Movement words to further stimulate these experiences would be: lengthy, extensive as against brief, short-term, protracted, transitory, fleeting, etc.

Sequences with emphasis on duration can be made by repeating movement patterns similar to the above and by adding changes in length of *pause,* etc.

To develop *rhythm,* students have to determine the speed and duration of each single movement as well as decide upon the length of pauses which separate one from the other. Pauses are as important in making movement phrases as punctuation is in language. They may indicate a transient rest like a comma, the finality of a full stop, the open-endedness of an interrogation mark or the special emphasis produced by an exclamation mark. Regular rhythms can be most easily experienced in single activities such as walking, skipping, galloping, etc., which have a natural even pulse. Irregular rhythms are created by free use of timing, e.g., two jumps, short pause, one jump, long pause, three jumps, stop. These patterns will only fully retain their irregular quality if no attempt is made to fit them into a metre or pulse. Such rhythms need to be performed with special precision as they have no set frame to hold them together.

Any rhythm is in itself a *sequence* and to develop them further one needs to add one rhythm to another. Groups or clusters of rhythmic sequences make up *phrases,* and a number of phrases becomes a movement study. There is no way of predicting how many phrases a study will contain as this depends entirely on the way the content of the chosen theme is being developed. Phrases of regular rhythms may lead to patterns such as are found in folk and society dances and occur more often when clearly structured music takes the lead.

Any aspect of the Time factor can in itself become a theme for improvisations and dances, e.g., Acceleration, Speed, or can be drawn upon when interpreting themes from "The World Around" and "The World Within".

Regular rhythms will feature more prominently in subjects such as Machines, Monotony;
Irregular rhythms in Volcanic Eruptions, Distractions;
Slow speed in Lava, Depression;
Quick speed in Lightning, Agitation.

29

(d) Dynamics

When looking at the relationship between Time and Force one is able to trace certain dynamic patterns which arise from the way in which Force is released. This may be *instantaneous*, in which case movements will start in a percussive manner and be carried on eagerly to completion. Against this, a *gradual* release of Force gives movements a lingering quality, produced by their being carried out without concern for duration. The vitality of Movement depends extensively on the fluctuations of these qualities. The use of Space and the degree of Fluency also play a part in Movement Dynamics—movements radiating from the body tend to feel more vivid than ingoing ones, and free flowing movements more lively than those which are controlled or restrained. Space and Fluency, however, we regard as additional features to Movement Dynamics and have omitted them from the groupings we propose for experiencing dynamic qualities.

Dynamic patterns

Grouping of Movements based on Dynamic qualities:

Force: *strong*; release: *gradual*—as expressed in movement words such as drag, squeeze, writhe, knead, pull

Force: *strong*; release: *instantaneous*—hit, kick, explode, thrash, whip, rip, stab, chop, grab, slap, burst, stamp

Force: *light*; release: *gradual*—drift, sail, float, melt, glide, wave, sneak, sink, rise, wilt, ooze, skate

Force: *light*; release: *instantaneous*—drip, shrug, flinch, flip, flick

Swinging is the result of a sudden impulse leading into a gradual action.

Vibratory movements are created through quick repetition of sudden actions, such as: flicker, drizzle, wobble, bubble, quiver, shudder, flutter, quake.

All these actions can be carried out by different Body Activities and varied with regard to speed, rhythm, Space and Fluency.

Development can take place in the usual manner by making groups or *sequences* containing the same type of Movement Dynamics, e.g., rip – stamp – kick, or glide – sink – rise. Interest can be added by sequencing movements of related or contrasting dynamic qualities, e.g., explode – float – drip, or flick – whip – stab. Transitions of this nature will be of great value for the discovery of the finer nuances of Movement Dynamics.

Most of these dynamic qualities can become themes in themselves, for example, Bubbles, Drizzle . . . or they can be drawn upon when interpreting themes from "The World Around" or "The World Within". Instantaneous actions will feature more prominently in War, Vivaciousness; gradual actions in Iceberg, Lagoon, Peace.

(e) Fluency

Any movement can be performed with a feeling either of *freedom* or of *restraint*. In fluent movements the experience will be one of being drawn along or carried away, while in those that are not a feeling of restriction will be dominant. Restrained movements will start reluctantly and their progress will be hesitant; they will show little variation in dynamic qualities and the use of Space will be inhibited. Fluent movements will, of course, have the opposite characteristics.

By offering students opportunities to experience the varying degrees of Fluency, they will be able to apply these at will when interpreting movement themes.

Fluency

Some suggestions for experiencing varying degrees of Fluency:

Fluent "running" can be contrasted with hesitant "walking"; free "rolling" with hesitant "creeping"; fluent gesture with hesitant turning. In addition to these contrasts, the Fluency aspect of Body Activities can also *increase* and *decrease* or *change abruptly* from abandon to stagnation.

Movement words which will stimulate actions carried out without hindrance or restraint of either a physical or psychological nature would be: abandoned, uncontrolled, eager, free. Words which contribute towards the experience of restraint would be: hesitant, controlled, reluctant, reticent, withheld, bridled.

Fluency in *sequences* will be characterised by easy or inhibited transitions between various Body Activities.

Any of the feeling-qualities expressed in the movement words listed above can become themes for improvisations and dances, e.g., Abandon, Control, Reticence.

Ideas which would draw on these movement experiences as material for their interpretation could be: Growth, The River, Obstacles, Freedom.

4 Topics

It has already been demonstrated in the preceding pages that themes for movement studies can arise from the simplest of movement practices. This is one way of stimulating creative expression through Movement. The other is to offer to students or let them bring forward topics they would wish to interpret in dance form, and help them to explore the various ways in which this can be done. As soon as topics are introduced, no matter from which angle, the orientation changes from the experiencing of Movement as such to Movement becoming a medium of expression. The focus will then be directed towards involving students in ideas and letting these act as the main source for movement inspiration. Any experimentation which takes place will centre around how best to express the chosen theme. Sensitive and varied movements become a means to an end—they no longer represent an end in themselves.

We believe that to dance about a topic can be as natural as to talk about it, draw, sculpt or sing it. With this in mind anything may be considered suitable, provided it can be perceived in terms of Movement. There is rarely justification in rejecting a theme presented in a movement lesson by either the teacher or the students; at times it may be difficult to see the possibilities a certain theme may offer, yet a discussion about it can open up new avenues of interpretation.

To make a selection from the unlimited range of topics easier, we have attempted to group them into three main areas: "Movement", "The World Around", and "The World Within". We realise that no clear-cut division exists between the three, as "The World Within", that is personality, is inseparable from "The World Around", environment, and "Movement" is part of both. We consider these groups to be effective guidelines for the purpose of teaching, yet wish to emphasise that no attempt should be made to interpret them in any other way.

Topics have to be within the reach of the students' understanding, depending on their maturity and experience. Any topic should be seen as a question for which the answer has to be found in Movement. The students' imagination may need supporting comments from the teacher, which may be expressed in terms such as: "Is there perhaps another way of 'saying' what you mean?", "Does this (particular movement) 'feel right' to you?", "Should you use more Space?", "Less speed?", etc. On the other hand, too many remarks may be restrictive to some students, for they may not have had sufficient time to explore one idea before another is suggested to them. In the main, however, students learn to disregard some of these comments and only use the ones that appear relevant to the movement task they are working on.

(a) Topics from within the Sphere of "Movement" Itself

Feeling the Dynamics of Movement in Space is in itself an exciting experience. The sensation of high leaps, fast runs, abrupt turns and slow sinking can create the desire to build a movement study around it. It is possible for any aspect of Movement, for example lightness, shapes, etc., to completely absorb the dancer's imagination and, together with the awareness of the movements of his body, become the main source for creativity. In the course of this creative process many new and original movements and movement combinations may evolve, all of which will lead to a new and personal interpretation of the given theme. Topics taken from Movement itself provide for experiences in which idea and material merge into one, without touching on areas which lie outside the sphere of Movement. From here

Towards the centre

students will find it easier to branch out and interpret other subjects, yet not lose awareness of the qualities inherent in Movement itself.

How each aspect of Movement can lead towards becoming an improvisation or dance study has already been discussed under the respective headings in the preceding chapters. We list them again so that they can be seen more clearly in the context of "Topics":

The Body:

—Body Awareness;
Body Activities *(locomotion, turning, elevation, falls, gesture)*.

Movement Principles:

—Space *(shapes and pathways)*;
—Force *(strength, lightness, heaviness, weight transference, balance, off balance)*;
—Time *(speed and rhythm)*;
Dynamics *(instantaneous or gradual release of Force, swinging, vibrations)*;
Fluency *(freedom, restraint)*.

Ideas for dancing drawn from the environment

(b) Topics from "The World Around"

The world is full of subjects that one can interpret in Dance, comprising all that can be seen, heard, tasted, smelled or touched. If the impression is mainly visual the interpretation of the shape or movement pattern observed can be fairly simple. On the other hand, the students' imagination may take them well beyond realistic interpretation and into the sphere of fantasy where, for instance, trees move around and cars dance. Dance studies on themes of this nature are best encouraged by the comment "can you feel yourself moving like (the model you observe)?" rather than "imagine yourself being . . .". Dancing, by being more symbolic, is a very different process from miming, which primarily aims at imitating. This does not rule out the fact that much can be learned from copying, for it requires close observation, leading to a greater understanding of the movements of a given subject. It also teaches one to be more precise as one is expected to adhere to the movement patterns of the model. Copying, used with discretion, can be a valuable addition to creative practices.

Sensations received through touch, taste or smell are more difficult to express in Movement, as in these instances the step from the one medium to the other is less direct and makes greater demands on the imagination. Sound, although in the same category, arouses immediate movement responses and can become quite spontaneously part of movement experience.

There is no specific way of grouping topics from "The World Around"; we, on the whole, follow the pattern of "People, Places, Events, Nature and Man-made Objects". Dancing about any of these will establish a more sensitive appreciation of the physical environment.

Suggestions for certain principles that can be adopted when
using impressions from "The World Around" as themes for Dance ideas:

Students can learn to identify with visual images by being made aware of
the movement qualities these contain. It requires repeated emphasis that the
movements observed need not be interpreted realistically. The dance of a
cat, for instance, may contain a far greater variety of movements than the
animal would actually make; a certain feline character has to be retained but
otherwise free scope should be given to the imagination.

It may appear "way out" to interpret a "penetrating smell", a "biting
taste" or a "hard grip", yet such topics have proved to be very popular and
stimulating. Movement studies arising from reactions to sensations are also
challenging, e.g., "shivering" when feeling cold, "shuddering" when
swallowing a bitter substance, "gliding" along in a cooling breeze.

Inexperienced students of any age may need guidance towards creating a
complete study on any of these topics and we suggest that the following
steps can be taken to assist them:

1. The use of a body shape or isolated Body Activity to interpret the
   chosen impression, e.g., taking on the shape of a "rock"; performing a
   gesture of rising and sinking like "smoke"; light running like "rain".
2. Exploration of other possible activities which could express the image:
   "rocks" can roll (locomotion on different body parts); "smoke" can
   circle (performed by gestures of the arms, legs, head, torso); "rain" can
   splash (interpreted through elevation).
3. This procedure can be followed up with simple *sequences*: the "rock"
   can roll and end in a shape—this can be done in many different ways;
   "smoke" can stretch high, sink to the floor, turn on the floor and
   return to standing (all this can be accompanied by a variety of arm
   gestures); "rain" can run lightly, interspersed with sudden jumps,
   changing directions, shapes in the air, etc.

We have found that graded practices give students confidence towards
dancing freely on any topic without either too much imitating or else running
out of movement ideas.

In the examples given so far, it was suggested that students identify with
some facets of "The World Around". To these can be added interpretations
of one's involvement in it or one's reactions to it, such as being "Trapped in
an Earthquake". The teacher can create the right atmosphere by pointing
out some details of what might happen in such a situation; for example,
buildings collapsing; the ground being split open; tidal waves swamping the
land, etc. On the lighter side, students may see themselves as taking part in
all kinds of fetes, carnivals, "pop" festivals, etc., in which they can represent
in Movement many different characters such as Men on Stilts, Jesters and
Pop Singers. All these topics lend themselves very easily to group involvement from which dance drama may develop.

In the course of students becoming more familiar with the language of
Movement, suggestions by the teachers can be reduced to a minimum and
offered only when it becomes apparent that, in a particular study, some sort
of stagnation point has been reached.

(c) Topics from "The World Within"

Themes from "The World Within" arise from the sphere of thoughts, emotions and fantasy, and give scope for expressing these inner experiences in Movement. They will result in very personal interpretations if no influence is exerted from the outside. The dancer will be mainly concerned with his feelings about the world that surrounds him, which his movement imagination will assist him to express. On the whole, the intellectual element in Dance is directed more towards the structuring of themes and the organisation of movement patterns. It seldom comes into play when Movement is first introduced and, if enforced, could inhibit creativity. More experienced students need to employ their intellectual faculties to work out the various aspects of form, while taking care not to force their movements into preconceived and, consequently, often rather stilted patterns.

The grouping of themes on the basis of their emotional, intellectual or intuitive origin would invite much justifiable criticism, as constant interaction takes place between these areas of the personality. We can merely suggest ways by which attention can be focused in turn on one or the other and so ensure that all are given an outlet through expression in Movement.

It is of great significance to realise that Movement can also create emotions. Rocking will evoke a feeling of tranquillity or reflection, lashing out a feeling of aggression; narrow movements may lead to tension, wide movements to a feeling of freedom and release. Dances which are based on any of the themes connected with "The World Within" bring Movement into close relation with psychology. A more detailed discussion will follow in Chapter 7.

Sadness

Suggestions for principles which may be adopted for the interpretation of themes from "The World Within":

Some students interpret these quite spontaneously and assistance may be needed simply to help them to develop form. Others need to be made aware of the type of movement which feelings can evoke, in order to be able to express them in dancing. It is of paramount importance for the teacher to realise how widely movement reactions differ from person to person. *Anger* may make some people feel tense and rigid and their movements hesitant and sustained. Others who "let fly" will want to dance wildly and freely. *Happiness* may lead some to tranquil movements and others to excited movements, and *grief* to an outburst of despair or a quiet dance of mourning. Greater depth of understanding for people can be gained if students allow themselves to experience feelings in ways that are different from their own. We consider facial expression to be a part of Movement experience, yet we feel that it should not be as dominant as it is in mime.

Young children frequently find it difficult to sustain a whole movement study on a theme from "The World Within", and a beginning can be made by choosing a gradual progression in the manner suggested for themes from "The World Around". A child will quite readily take on a stance or perform an isolated Body Activity, e.g., "sitting sadly", "stamping angrily" or "jumping excitedly". This can be followed up with short *sequences*, e.g., a "sad walk ending in a sad sinking", a "happy whirling—running and jumping—ending with a gesture of welcome".

At times older students, too, may need this kind of easing into emotional themes before gaining sufficient courage to become fully involved in them.

The interpretation of complex feelings, e.g., "suspicion", fluctations of emotions, e.g., "from trust to suspicion to anger", or a gradual development like the "awakening of consciousness" are difficult to interpret and require a mature approach. The same would apply to topics drawing on abstract ideas, e.g., "existence" and "inferiority". All these themes necessitate a fluent command of the language of Movement and are usually beyond the scope of inexperienced students.

Experimenting with properties

(d) Topics stimulated through the Use of Properties

We have found that the use of properties such as scarves, balloons, hoops, etc., can add interest to the experience of certain movement qualities. Touching and handling materials that are light can bring about a more distinct feeling for buoyant movements, whilst the use of hoops directs the attention towards the design created in Space.

Students have stated that the shape, texture, and sometimes the colour of an object will influence Movement and promote unusual ideas. Often the property one works with takes on a particular meaning and becomes the centre for dramatic situations.

Properties will establish links between partners, and may make the experience of working together less personal by, at the same time, acting as a buffer. They also set a frame which both limits and concentrates the students' explorations and may initiate and direct movements into more original patterns. On occasions, properties can be felt as a tie, in which case it will be advisable to put off the planned experiment and wait for a time when students are likely to be more receptive to it.

Properties can also be effective in creating an atmosphere for story telling in Movement. Students may wish to interpret different roles and by interacting with each other will create a dance drama.

(Any properties or materials used in Creative Movement situations should first be tested for safety.)

Suggestions for the use of properties:

The list of properties we present below as being suitable for dancing is by no means complete. We hope that teachers will add their own ideas to it and also think of new and exciting ways of using the various materials. Perhaps, at the same time, it would be well to sound a warning that too many properties brought in too frequently may over stimulate some groups and lead to confusion, or have the opposite effect and rather stultify their movement experience.

Balloons can be integrated effectively into dances on the topics of Body Awareness and Floating. They may be seen as loved or hated objects, to be either worshipped or destroyed respectively.

Hoops invariably take on a symbolic meaning and may become the focal point of ritual dances.

Rods may simply lead to more architectural dances and also invite some kind of symbolism.

Scarves, through their texture, promote topics from within Movement such as Flexibility; or they may be used as masks in Hold-Ups or Harem Girls.

Larger pieces of materials if danced with will lead to movement topics containing slow and gradual movements, as perhaps in Clouds, Water, or if used as cloaks, skirts, hoods, etc., result in dances of Matadors, Magicians, Cloak-and-Dagger Men. Carrying them as canopies or hanging them as drapes will provide rather colourful settings.

Boxes can represent such widely differing objects as flowerpots, cocoons, or spaceships; they can be felt as a restricting cage or be as cosy as a nest.

Rostrums or platforms provide changes in levels, and contribute interesting angles for dances built round "Space" topics as well as scenery for royal courts, bases for statues, or platforms for meeting places.

Rusty pieces of metal can become the starting point for a movement drama on the topic of Shipwreck.

A metronome provides the ticking of a timeclock which can be used for the topic Highjacking or any scenes connected with gangsters.

There is hardly any piece of property which would not stir the imagination towards inventing interesting and original topics for Movement.

5 Planning the Programme

(a) General Comments

Any Creative Movement lesson needs to be looked at from the point of view of what it can offer in the way of movement experience. This also applies to lessons centring on a topic from "The World Around" or "The World Within", as their content too will have to be expressed and worked through by means of Movement. Whether a plan fulfils this condition can be established by testing it with the aid of the basic movement principles, a method which we refer to as movement analysis.

Creative Movement is often associated with practices such as "being a tree", which invariably result in students remaining on one spot and waving their arms from side to side. This interpretation could at best be classified as an attempt at mime, but certainly not as an experience in Creative Movement. If the content of a programme of this or any other nature is prepared with the aid of movement analysis, the result in the case of the "tree" would be as follows:

Trunk	*Branches*	*Leaves*
Space: Covering short distances, i.e., restricted	Covering longer distances but still rather contained	Free use of pathways leading into different directions, different angles, etc.
Force: Strong	Lighter	Very light
Time: Slow and steady	Speed and Dynamics more variable	Maximum variety of speed and Dynamics, e.g., vibratory movements, alternating with gradual ones, etc.
Fluency: Restrained	Tending to become looser	Very free

Having made this analysis one can interpret the "tree" by using a wide range of Body Activities to express the movement qualities it contains,

44

e.g., the trunk with strong, restricted and steady movements; the leaves lightly, with free use of Space and changing Dynamics. Provided these movement qualities are retained, any movement will be appropriate and need not be confined to re-creating the actual situation. The branches, for instance, can make intertwining pathways involving the whole body and covering all the available Space—they need not stay attached to the trunk. The movement of leaves can be interpreted with gestures of the legs and feet, with the weight supported on different body parts, changing levels, progressing by rolling, sliding, etc.

If the subject is Caterpillars, light wriggling, twisting, gliding, rising, sinking, etc., can take the body anywhere in Space and crawling along the floor will only be one of many movement variations. The same goes for Fishes which certainly do not have to remain at the bottom of the sea but can perform fish-like movements anywhere in Space.

Movement analysis is instrumental in freeing Movement from being imitative and therefore allows for a much more imaginative and original interpretation of any theme.

Group involvement

Responses of groups, as well as of individuals, differ very widely; consequently any guidelines given for planning have to be kept in very general terms. If teachers are in command of their subject and understand the needs of their students with regard to their physical, mental and emotional maturity, they should see no need to be given a step by step programme for teaching. An illustration of all the aspects we consider to be the foundations of Creative Movement has been given in the Movement Dial. To introduce these aspects to a group, no matter what age, appears to take about one lesson per week over a period of one academic year. The duration of these lessons will vary between about fifteen minutes for pre-school and sub-primary children, to thirty to forty-five minutes for children from eight to fourteen years, and anything up to one and a half hours for older groups who show a specific interest in Creative Movement. Additional time spent on practice within one year will enable students to acquire a wider range of experiences, but does not on the whole provide greater depth of understanding as this cannot be hurried along. Development can only be achieved by repeated experimentation with the same task in many different guises over a considerable period of time and not just in the course of a single lesson. Emphasis in the early stages is on breadth of experience, to which precision and refinement can only be added later.

Each lesson should be based on the requirements of the class, while at the same time sight must not be lost of the overall picture of Movement. With this in mind, planning of successive lessons will arise from the way students succeed in coping with the tasks given to them in any one lesson. If, for instance, students do not make effective use of Force, the content of the following lesson will be directed towards filling in this gap. Because students are allowed to solve tasks in their own way, any programme presented to young children will prove to be equally suitable for all age groups, the condition being that the teacher adjusts his attitude, language and expectancy to the age and experience of the students concerned. As mentioned previously, there are some topics which will be too demanding for some groups and should not be offered until a certain level of skill and understanding has been reached. Lessons should always be imaginative and a challenge to the students' creative abilities, and teachers should never stop searching for new ways of making this possible.

Students should be given complete freedom as to how they interpret a given topic. Guidance from the teacher should be directed towards making them clarify their own movements with regard to the way they use their bodies and apply basic movement principles. As students are not taught any specific steps, there is no need to be concerned about overtaxing physical and intellectual abilities. Some students, however, need encouragement to extend themselves over and above what they have already mastered, others provide their own challenge to reach a higher standard; a teacher needs to be aware of all these processes to be able to conduct a group successfully.

46

Planning needs to be tested over a period of time before a teacher can determine which approach is best for him as well as for the group he is taking. A programme may be unsuccessful for a number of reasons and not only because the plan was in itself a poor one; it may simply have been wrong to present it to a certain group at a particular point in time, or else it may have been presented in an uninspiring way. Plans definitely require preparation but need not be strictly adhered to. Students frequently develop interesting ideas which, although not related to the proposed topic, provide valuable experiences. It is not necessary to be concerned that such deviations can become disruptive because, if they do not lead anywhere, the teacher has his own plan to fall back on.

It may also happen that teachers think of more interesting ways of presenting their material on the spur of the moment, and they should not be afraid of using these in preference to what they had previously prepared.

(b) Basic Structure

The programme structure we suggest has proved to be an effective framework for planning lessons. It holds together the material one wishes to present and will assist in a more systematic evaluation.

Step 1. Introduction:	A physical and mental preparation for the Main Theme. The tasks may be presented in a structured manner by the teacher or developed more spontaneously with the students.
Step 2. Main Theme:	Exploration of, and experimentation with, certain prepared material which will include varied and/or contrasting movement qualities for the interpretation of the given topic.
Step 3. Second Subject:	This should enrich the Main Theme as well as bring in another point of interest. It may be advisable not to demand so much effort from students in dealing with the Second Subject and allow for a freer and less concentrated approach to it.
Step 4. Conclusion:	In rounding off the tasks set during the session, the conclusion should give students a sense of completion.

Any programme needs sufficient flexibility to allow for incidentals anywhere within and between the steps set out.

The content of the lesson plans which we include should be treated as samples which, in view of what we have stated, may not be applicable in their existing form to any one group.

1. Introduction: Awareness of different parts of the torso will be encouraged through practices of rocking, rolling and sliding on them. In addition, backs can be stretched, arched and bent, chest and ribs expanded, the whole trunk rotated, etc.

2. Main Theme: Awareness of feet. Practices will include standing on and moving along on the balls of the feet "lightly on toes", and on the whole foot through "stamping", and on heels, which might lead to an incidental practice of all kinds of humorous locomotion.
Further awareness of feet can be attained by pointing with them, and also hopping or skipping on them in various ways. This theme could in itself be concluded with a "dance of feet".

3. Second Subject: Awareness of hands. Experiments will be made with various hand gestures with emphasis on the awareness of palms, backs of hands and fingers. Practices can be extended to include arms which, when spread, may perform wing-like movements and suggest a dance of "winged creatures".

4. Conclusion: The lesson could end on a humorous note with full body involvement in a "dance of unexpected movements".

1. Introduction: Exploration of the maximum variety of locomotion, stressing the fact that all of it is a means of progressing from one position on the floor to another.

2. Main Theme: Gesture, performed by taking up a stance on feet, knees, etc., and moving only head, trunk and arms, to which may be added the body gesture of rising and sinking. From this may arise the imagery of Snakes or Wire-sculptures, etc.

3. Second Subject: Introduction of turns performed on different levels using variations in speed, and joined together by means of a variety of transitions.

4. Conclusion: Locomotion, gesture, and turning, woven into movement patterns, expressing whatever mood these suggest.

More advanced students would be expected to create repeatable sequences and to clarify each movement as well as the transitions between them.

1. Introduction: Wide and Narrow. Explored with wide swings, wide circles, alternating with narrow "cutting" movements performed with different body parts—wide stretching as against tight contractions.

2. Main Theme: Action and Reaction. Students will work out short phrases of body activities representing different types of questions, emphatic statements, attacks, retreats. The messages expressed in these statements would become evident by the way they are being terminated, e.g., in a questioning or exclamatory manner, etc.

3. Second Subject: Students now use similar sequences for Movement Conversations with each other. They may arrange the nature of the conversation beforehand or let it evolve in the course of dancing. Out of this may arise improvised partner or group studies in angry, humorous, gentle moods, etc.

4. Conclusion: The teacher or one of the students may conduct group movement performed in unison to round off the session with a feeling of coherence.

This example would be suitable for a more advanced class.

1.	Introduction:	Gestures, emphasising air patterns including curves, straight lines, dots, etc., leading into floor patterns performed by locomotion which may meander, zig-zag, make loops, etc.
2.	Main Theme:	Shapes. This task could begin with students taking on any one body shape then changing it to a related or contrasting one such as from tall to medium to small, from curved to spiky. The curved shape may then proceed by rolling, the spiky one by stepping and hopping, etc., and either can be performed in turning. Through elevation, shapes can be experienced in the air and either retained or changed on landing.
3.	Second Subject:	Shapes could be further characterised through changes in Dynamics, and sufficiently experienced students may be asked to group them into phrases.
4.	Conclusion:	Improvisations on topics such as Painting or Carving Space, using the experiences in shapes and patterns acquired in the session.

A central theme of Narrow and Wide may lead to a more dramatic conclusion, as for instance Confined, Free. Any theme can be related to partners and groups, which again introduces new angles of interpretation such as shapes "attacking" each other or groups confined within a small area of Space "interacting" with others who use Space freely.

The basic attributes of Force are best explored in connection with the basic attributes of Time, which will result in a variety of dynamic qualities.

1. Introduction: Light, percussive, and vibratory movements for warming up, contrasted with strong gradual stretching of different parts of the body incorporating weight transference.

2. Main Theme: The quality of the strong gradual introductory movements will be drawn upon to express the imagery of Magnetism which gives scope to the experience of being attracted and repulsed from various points in Space, with different body parts leading the movements. This topic of Magnetism lends itself well to partner work with students creating various ways of moving towards and away from each other, with specific emphasis on contrasts between gradual and sudden movement-qualities. Progression on various body parts producing changes of levels may add further interest to this practice.

3. Second Subject: This will centre around the topic of Electricity, making use of the percussive and vibratory movements practised in the Introduction and developing them into sequences of "flickering", "quivering", "darting" of sparks in combination with the steady flow of an electric current. All movements of the Second Subject would freely cover wide areas of Space, contrasting with those of the Main Theme which would have followed along clearly defined pathways.

4. Conclusion: Main Theme and Second Subject together could form the basis for a movement improvisation on science fiction for which some record or tape of electronic music could be used to set the atmosphere.

"On and off balance"—another aspect of Force—could be substituted for Magnetism as a Main Theme, which may lead to a more humorous ending.

1. Introduction: Selected Body Activities performed with variable speed, e.g., slow stepping—fast turning, making a variety of floor patterns. Accelerating gestures whilst standing would provide an effective warm-up for torso and arms.

2. Main Theme: Creating rhythmic sequences of Body Activities which should now include also elevation and falls—the sequences to be of different duration, e.g., an accelerated short run leading into a jump and fall, pause, slow turn on floor level, and very slow rising.

3. Second Subject: Some sequences to be joined into small clusters of three to five, representing topics like Primitive Rain Dance or Escape.

4. Conclusion: Free groupings of movements with less accentuated rhythms in a quiet and solemn key such as in Sun Worship or Repose.

Topics dealing with the element of Time often invite quite spontaneous sound accompaniment by means of body percussion or through using drums, rhythm sticks, and, for the more measured rhythms, gong beats or droning. Recorded primitive or Eastern music may also provide an effective background.

The element of Time forms a major link between Movement and Sound—it will be enlarged upon in Chapter 6.

1. Introduction: Fluent, uncontrolled, warming up by using a selected number of Body Activities alternating with sudden stops. These should take place on different levels to improve flexibility.

2. Main Theme: "Going through a maze" using a great variety of cautiously performed movements of restricted height and width, expressing anxiety such as may be experienced in a nightmare. (Students have to be reminded that a topic of this nature is not to be interpreted in mime, which means that they also experiment with Body Activities that would be unusual in such situations, viz., narrow turns, high balancing movements, sliding on the back.) This topic may develop into an interesting group activity of one student leading the way and all other group members following in line formation, zig-zagging, meandering, spiralling, etc., with everybody going along the same path but using his own ideas for locomotion. The progression would be hesitant right through and could come to a complete standstill in the end.

3. Second Subject: The stationary group could gradually dissolve with group members detaching themselves singly, or two and three at a time, their movements taking on a free flowing quality, reaching out high, far, and wide, expressing Release.

4. Conclusion: Creating an open group shape with rounded contours and leaving a great deal of Space between group members. While students take up a definite stance, movement may continue by means of gentle gesturing like a very large mobile moving lightly in a breeze.

Programmes which lean on partner work are not suitable for young children. To introduce Fluency to the lower age groups the above plan could be used, leaving out all formations and concentrating on the quality of movements as expressed by individual students.

Example of a Movement Programme on the topic of "Building" (from "The World Around")

1. Introduction: Mixing, mincing, rotating gestures, using all body parts (as if in a giant concrete mixer). These could alternate with jerky movements of stones, and the "splashing" of water.

2. Main Theme: "Pouring" of concrete, which involves slow, gradual, forceful movements going along clearly defined pathways and ending in all kinds of forceful shapes. These shapes can "crack" and "crumble", and eventually be re-formed into the same or a different shape. (Students need to be reminded that shapes can be formed with the weight resting on different body parts, which will add a great deal of variety.)

3. Second Theme: Free light floating movements of dust particles, bringing in all the Body Activities which would not have been used in the Main Theme, such as running and light jumps combined with gestures and turns, covering much Space and finally landing gently on the ground.

4. Conclusion: From the floor position, working towards a construction of Concrete and Steel, finding different links with partners and making sure that all members of the group are connected with each other in some way. The final position would be strong and could feel powerful.

These could centre around the machinery displayed, the animals, the people who visit the show, the sideshows, etc.

We will briefly sketch the possible development of the first two topics, as it should be no problem to construct any of the others along the same lines.

MACHINERY:

1. Introduction: Oiling, e.g., maximum variety of gliding movements as if going up and down narrow tubes, etc.
2. Main Theme: Experimentation with machine-like movements, e.g., wheels, pistons, hammers, conveyor belts, etc., and working a number of them into a sequence.
3. Second Subject: Selecting a partner whose sequence combines well with one's own and modifying these sequences to create a joint pattern; for instance, fitting together like "clockwork".
4. Conclusion: Springs, e.g., experimentation with all kinds of bobbing and bouncing until the spring "breaks" and falls to the ground.

THE ANIMALS:

1. Introduction: Light "pecking", tapping, fluttering movements of "chickens".
2. Main Theme: Jumping, bucking, kicking, twisting, rolling like horses at the rodeo.
3. Second Subject: Heavy, slow movements, like those of cattle grazing.
4. Conclusion: A quiet settling with an occasional "swishing", rolling or turning.

It will be necessary to remind students again that the medium for expression is Creative Movement, not mime, and therefore all topics should be interpreted through free and imaginative dance movements based on the results of movement analysis.

Example of a Movement Programme on Moods (from "The World Within")
designed for a school situation

---

1. Introduction: Starting from a discussion on the different ways
people feel—sad, happy, angry . . .—children will use
different gestures to interpret these; e.g., "sad
hands", "greedy fingers", "proud backs", "angry
feet", "funny tummies", etc.
(This practice can even be done with children sitting
in their desks.)

2. Main Theme: Experimentation with a variety of Body Activities
expressing moods, e.g., "sad walks", "happy gyra-
tions", "angry jumps", "funny falls" . . . which can
lead to short sequences, provided the children are
mature enough to cope with such tasks.

3. Second Subject: Children divide into groups, each choosing and
interpreting a mood agreed upon between themselves.
They end their dancing in a group shape expressing
the respective moods.

4. Conclusion: A "quiet" mood, possibly set by bringing in some
suitable music and letting the children take on
positions of relaxation.

As children have a free choice of moods they may possibly work through
some emotional tensions in such a session.

It will be evident that the same programme with minor adaptation can be
presented to any age group.

Example of a Movement Programme on "Confusion" and "Clarity" ("The World Within") which could be presented to a fairly mature and advanced group

1. Introduction: A set of tasks designed to improve the skills of the particular group in question. Some emphasis will be placed on clarity of performance.

2. Main Theme: Confusion: students will first experiment with different dance movements which express this feeling, such as turns (not knowing where to turn to) and locomotion, interspersed with abrupt stops and changes of direction (changing one's mind). The teacher may decide to ask students to perform some of these movements while balancing in order to extend their skills and range of movements. Elevation or falls may be asked for to express moments of despair. After having completed a number of experiments, students may be required to combine some selected movements into a short statement about some aspect of Confusion.

3. Second Subject: Clarity: students will now direct their attention towards clearly designed movement sequences. They may not be requested to make them repeatable, as the quality of Movement will be slow and controlled and clear patterns can emerge spontaneously in the course of the improvisation.

4. Conclusion: Not every lesson needs to include group work. The above topics may now be drawn together and it can be suggested that students progress gradually from Clarity to Confusion, or vice versa. Should students wish to work together, it could be suggested that all but one of the group represent a state of Confusion and one dancer, through the quality of his movements, bring in Clarity; the reverse is equally possible.

Alternative topics for this plan could be Peace and War and, for less mature students, Summer and Winter. A lesson of this nature would take one to one and a half hours. Suitable musical accompaniment could only be provided by a musician who can follow the moods of the dancers, or else the teacher himself may wish to devise appropriate sound mixtures for contrast; some sections can be done in silence.

1. Introduction: Waking Up through stretching, led by different body parts into different directions. For experienced groups this can be done in a systematic fashion using limbs, trunk and head in isolation as well as in some specific combinations. This may alternate with some organised swinging to release the tension and loosen the joints.

2. Main Theme: Each student creates spatial patterns by manipulating the hoop in as many ways as possible, by adapting and/or contrasting the roundness of its shape.

3. Second Subject: Hoops can be placed on the floor and used to make pathways around them, alternating with leaps into the centre of the hoop. Students can move in this way from one hoop to another, which will further vary the floor patterns.

4. Conclusion: Students may decide on some meaning that the hoop may have for them and use this as a basis for an improvisation around it.

Some students may wish to accompany others on suitable instruments. If the topic is of sufficient interest to a group the students may decide to compose a dance study over a number of lessons.

Similar programmes can be built around other properties.

(d) Long-range Planning

Within the framework of any long-range planning, students should be given the opportunity to develop their talents as extensively as possible and should be assisted to progress at a rate that suits their needs.

Initially, students will find it rewarding if a given task is fulfilled with imagination and feeling but with little regard to form. As they gain experience, the students will concern themselves more with the quality of their interpretations and of necessity become more discerning in their choice of movements. By this stage the grouping of movements will be an almost intuitive process and the students' interest can be directed towards refinement of individual movements as well as of the transitions between them. More intricate work will demand a more proficient and skilful use of the body and a more conscious approach to form and dynamics. This too applies to partner and group work which, with increasing complexity, requires a more skilful adaptation between group members. A great deal more will be learned about all facets of Movement listed on the Movement Dial as students progress through these stages of development.

If we were to adapt the programme from "The World Around" on "Building" to a more advanced student group, we could see this being done in the following manner:

Introduction: Students would be required to become more specific as to which body part performs the "jerking", "rotating" and "splashing" movements; to determine precisely where a movement is to begin, which pathway it follows, where it terminates, the amount of Force it involves, etc.; and see that co-ordination is achieved between the various actions.

Main Theme: When interpreting the "pouring of concrete", one might expect students to create one or more fully clarified and repeatable sequences of movements and that these should lead to a group shape which is definite in its points of contact, line and tension.

Second Subject: "Dust" would provide opportunities for less concentrated work but one would expect a greater degree of lightness and flexibility in Space.

Conclusion: The final "settling" of the dust whether individually or in groups should give evidence of better control over the body when sinking to the floor and a more conscious movement-relationship to others.

The two themes and the conclusion of the programme could together become the source of a movement study on "Building". This may develop into an organised improvisation, the general pattern of which would be sufficiently set to be made repeatable. Alternatively, students may choose to structure the themes into a dance in which both movements and patterns are consistent. In both instances, the integration of a variety of aids such as slides, film, sound, drapes, properties, etc., may enrich the experience and set off the work more distinctly.

All programmes can be dealt with in a similar manner and, in addition to this, students may find their own ways of setting themselves higher goals. Such possibilities should always be left open so that no procedure within Creative Movement teaching becomes standardised.

One cannot expect all students within a group to reach the same standard; for those who wish to go further, the scope is very wide. Students who have over a period of years exhausted the possibilities within the class situation may wish to choreograph solo and group dances or dance dramas, and seek opportunities to present these on stage. Others may work towards becoming members of existing dance companies or else undergo training as special teachers in Creative Movement. However, our main concern within the framework of this book is to promote enjoyment, understanding and respect for all that Creative Movement has to offer, and to give students an understanding of themselves and others which may well be of value in many different situations.

PERFORMING

For many students the experience of Movement may be intensified through sharing it with others who are not participating. If students are motivated by an honest desire to do this, dance presentations may well add a new and valuable dimension to their work. For a dancer to feel that he is getting his message across and making contact with his audience will enable him to present what he wishes to communicate with greater conviction. This kind of "performing" fulfils a definite purpose which will not be achieved if students are allowed to "show off". Technique is a means of presenting content which must be formulated in a way that makes it intelligible to a reasonably perceptive audience. Performing is a responsible task; it requires a sense of purpose, talent, and at least an adequate mastery of one's material. Those who wish to earn the privilege of presenting their ideas to others have to do this through concentrated work; improvisations are seldom successful as a means of communication unless the audience can be made to participate in some active way. If this is not intended, it seems essential to have formulated one's message prior to its presentation. It cannot be avoided that performers sometimes cannot work up the right spirit, but if the content of their presentation is meaningful and its form clear, the audience will nevertheless be able to gain a good deal from watching it.

62

(e) Evaluation

Teachers will evaluate how students have coped with the various movement tasks by applying the principles inherent in Movement as criteria for evaluation. Each lesson will contain one or more objectives depending on the experience the group has previously acquired. If, for instance, the programme outlined for "Space" were presented to beginners, their undivided attention would be given to creating shapes (the content of the Main Theme), and they would find it difficult to clarify any additional aspects or cope with any other particular skill. Evaluation at this stage would then be concerned with this one aspect, and teachers would assist the students in succeeding with the given task by suggesting ways of making shapes "complete" by more fully involving all parts of their bodies. (This does not imply that the teacher attempts to change the students' ideas, but rather he helps them to improve the quality of their interpretation.)

As students become more experienced several other objectives would be added to this major one of shape. For example, students would be expected to clarify the Force and Dynamics of a particular sequence of shapes and also use more advanced skills, e.g., shapes in elevation or while turning on one foot, and other more challenging movement combinations. It may be necessary to teach some technical points so that students can overcome certain difficulties in performing the type of movement they have in mind.

All lessons need a similar analysis; if, for example, the content is rhythm, then evaluation will be concerned with how well students are able to define the rhythmical structure of their movements; if the development of a lesson turns to sequencing then assessment will be concerned with the quality of transitions; if a topic was chosen from "The World Around" or "The World Within", one would look for how well the content of the given topic was expressed in Movement. Interpretation of an idea, whatever it may be, will be demonstrated through the quality and imaginative use of movements which evolve in this creative situation.

The skill and the level of understanding of any group will determine the objectives set for a particular lesson. Teachers can vary the number of goals they wish to attain in one programme; this is one of the reasons why one programme can be directed to different levels.

Much of the success of a lesson depends on the involvement of the students and the enjoyment they gain from the experience. Although this may occur, teachers should still question whether the group reached the movement objectives set. Their observations of students will show them how to follow up the programme and how to help individual students to extend themselves and to obtain better results. Sometimes the way individual students or a group react will provide a pointer to areas which need further and more careful exploration. Response to group work may indicate that further practices in this area are required to give greater cohesion and understanding between the members of the group. In the course of a lesson students may be encouraged to evaluate each other's work and this will give them a greater understanding of what is required to complete a task successfully. By using the basic movement principles as criteria for evaluation they can gradually learn to assess their own achievements. There is no set "scale" by which progress of students can be determined—teachers must construct their own for each programme and for each group.

(f) Summary of Teaching Points

Many teaching points have been touched upon in the preceding text, but by drawing them together we feel that an over-all picture can be obtained.

Whatever stage of development has been reached, teachers should always offer suggestions to make the experience of Movement more challenging and exciting, without stifling the students' own ideas.

Teachers may illustrate certain points with impromptu movements to serve as suggestions for the solution of the given task and then allow the students to work it out for themselves. There is no need to be afraid that students may fall into the habit of copying, for this may, in many cases, be of advantage in the early stages of experience. If properly guided, students will soon discover their own resources and will be able to experiment with Movement by themselves. In Creative Movement, which is oriented towards diversification rather than uniformity, there is little room for teaching and demonstrating set steps and routines. Teachers who use this method tend to impose their own style of moving upon a student group and so inhibit the development of originality.

Programmes can centre around a variety of stimuli, e.g., poems, pictures, percussion instruments, and other teaching aids. The teacher's voice, the movement words used and the incidental comments made will help set the atmosphere and add additional stimulation to the creative process. It must be remembered again that too much stimulation may defeat its purpose and that too rapid a change from one task to another can make students feel frustrated, as they need time to develop their own ideas.

To encourage progress, the teacher has to look at each student as an individual, but should not lose sight of the progress of the group as a whole. There will be common as well as individual goals to attain, none of which can be set without observation and analysis of the potentials of the group. The rate of progress of each student as well as that of the group should be assessed regularly to ensure that everyone continues to work at full capacity.

64

Programming, in the main, consists of a progression of tasks within certain frames, all giving scope to the students to use their own imagination and capabilities. Frames, far from being restrictive, seem to produce a greater concentration of effort and prevent students from going off on tangents.

Consideration should be given to balancing Movement against moments of stillness. Activity and rest are both a part of movement teaching, for a moment of rest prepares students for the task at hand and a pause after any movement or phrase gives a sense of completion. Every movement has a root, a pathway and a point of termination. Each phrase, like a sentence, has a beginning, a development and an ending.

All tasks will touch upon a number of areas of Movement and only vary through change of emphasis. This must be kept in mind in all Creative Movement teaching. Basically, the methods of teaching Movement remain the same irrespective of the maturity of the student group. The volume of material that can be drawn upon is large enough to allow appropriate selection for any level.

6 Movement in Relation to Sound and Other Areas of Art and Learning

It is an advantage if a teacher does not see his own subject in isolation but is adequately informed as to the borders it shares with other areas. This, we believe, will make it possible to establish relevant links between the different sections of the curriculum.

(a) Movement and Sound

Within the sphere of creative expression, Sound could well be considered the closest relative to Movement. Both are a spontaneous response to feelings and a basic means of communication. They have many elements in common, for example, fluency, dynamics, speed and, specifically, rhythm, which appears to be the driving force behind them both. However, observations over the last few years have shown that students become more aware of the qualities inherent in Movement itself if music is not taking a leading part in movement practices. If music is not used, students invariably attempt to relate Movement directly to themselves. This releases them from the dependence on music which has existed in the field of Dance for so long, and directs the focus of concentration on what we see as being the true material for Dance.

In practical terms of teaching it is very important that students express their own innate feeling for rhythm and that this should be given scope for development. Learning about rhythms by matching existing sound patterns is a valuable experience in movement discipline and, from the point of view of teaching music, it assists in absorbing rhythm more fully. When teaching Movement, however, it is of primary importance that students learn to create their own rhythmical patterns. Young children, in particular, find keeping time with the music quite difficult and, should it be demanded, are inclined to concentrate on this aspect more than on the actual movement experience. For instance, if children are asked to skip in time with a given beat, it might impede the quality of their elevation; it could be that the beat will be too fast for those who can jump high or far, and too slow for those who cannot. For the sake of experiencing elevation to the full, it is suggested that the teacher allow children and adults to choose their own speed and rhythm even in such practices as galloping, "bunny hops", "frog jumps", etc.; it requires a good deal more skill to perform these to an existing rhythmical pattern. We therefore advocate unstructured spontaneous sound accompaniment which fits the theme and blends in with the given movement task without dictating its rhythmical progression.

Both children and adults, if not discouraged, will make their own variety of Sound to accompany Movement by clapping, stamping and other body percussion as well as chanting and other vocal sounds. They should also learn to find suitable instruments with which to accompany each other's movements and both "dancer" and "musician" should decide on how the Sound and Movement can be combined. The teacher's voice, too, is a most important sound instrument, as are the words he chooses to emphasise various movement qualities. All this, we believe, establishes the truest and most basic relationship between the two disciplines.

Movement and Sound can complement each other in a most satisfying manner, providing that they are combined sensitively and with understanding towards a common goal. We fully recognise that Sound is very stimulating to movement experience and we encourage it to be used, provided that no dependence is established and the experience of the dancer remains centred in Movement itself.

Structured music, live or recorded, does not have to be matched or followed; it can be conversed with, contrasted, etc., or merely used to set the atmosphere. Compositions which do not contain a conventional rhythmic and melodic line but rather place the emphasis on tone quality are more suitable for dancing. Music of this kind can be found amongst the compositions of contemporary musicians, who are often concerned with new tone combinations either of conventional instruments or of electronic and other sound-making equipment. Similar sound mixtures can be created spontaneously as a background for Creative Movement, and a wide range of equipment should be available for both teacher and students.

Instruments which can be explored in a number of ways are: gongs, cymbals, Indian hand cymbals, finger cymbals, all types of drums, tambours, tambourines, temple blocks, castanets, guiros, ratchets, rhythm sticks, sandpaper blocks, etc.

If used in more than just the usual way they can produce a very wide range of Sound. To these more basic instruments can be added the glocken-spiel, autoharps, zithers, and harmonicas, which allow for a greater variation in pitch. There is no need to attempt the playing of conventional melodies or harmonies but rather to let the students experiment in finding sound combinations which will fit in with their movement studies. The piano, if used imaginatively, will provide a wealth of Sound for creating moods; strings can be brushed or plucked, hit with a soft drum stick and even the frame can be used for "drumming". Other interesting means of sound-making are: tapping bottles, crumpling paper, tinkling or clattering of metallic objects, whistles, sirens, etc. Such accompaniment, far from being chaotic, often produces very sensitive as well as dynamic sound effects and may capture a given movement quality more effectively than existing musical compositions.

(b) Movement and Other Areas of Art and Learning

These other areas, we believe, can be seen in two different ways: one in which Movement is used as an adjunct to illustrate certain aspects of a subject, and the other where the common elements of a subject are being discovered and explored. The former would consist of representing in Movement the scene of a painting, the content of a story or an existing sculpture. The latter would consist of arranging groupings of students to correspond with sets in mathematics, action and reaction in science, or enabling them to become alert to the body involvement necessary when creating shapes of letters in writing. Such practices can "liven up" and add interest to the material under discussion and make the experience more real. Alternatively, dancing about a topic first may result in a more animated interpretation of it in language, art or science.

One can easily see Movement as a means of understanding many subjects in the curriculum. In social studies, much can be gained by learning the folk dances of different nations, as this will acquaint students with the national characteristics which are invariably reflected in them.

One should not overlook the significance of today's social dances which, like folk dances of the past, give an insight into the relationships of young people in our society. History too can become more real by creating movement pageants which would represent the life of people in different eras.

Drama practices can evolve from movement improvisations if words are added spontaneously—in fact many contemporary drama teachers develop their subject in this way. The quality of speech is itself governed by fluctuations of volume and through rhythm (punctuation and the placing of accents). These, as well as the degree of fluency speech contains, are also

68

structural components of Movement, and we maintain that they would be better understood if experienced in both media. Language includes a number of words which describe movement qualities and frequently one is not aware that one uses them when explaining other concepts: the "uneven rhythm" of a poem, a "balanced" sentence, the "sweeping lines" of a picture or building, an *andante* (a "walking" pace) in music, etc. The movement teacher uses a large number of movement words and, by grasping their meaning physically, students will be able to understand their meaning better when they come across them in other subjects. Discovering such links in language will help to reveal the structural relationships that exist between different areas, and this, according to Professor J. S. Bruner (1965), establishes an essential basis for the learning process.

Scientific concepts concerned with motion can often be assimilated better through moving; for example, the pathways and changing movement characteristics of molecules within solids, liquids and gases; the movement of cells and the chromosomes within these, etc. With regard to nature study such concepts as metamorphosis and mimicry will become more meaningful.

The basic concepts of mathematics may be formed more easily if students are given the opportunity to make shapes with their bodies, and to work with properties such as circles, triangles and squares, etc. Quantity, density, size, height, and other aspects of mathematics can all be better integrated while being experienced in Movement.

Spatial relationships which are of great importance to a sculptor will have much in common with those of the dancer. The present development of sculpture towards kinetic art makes this relationship with Dance even more pronounced. In a painting, line and the distribution of colours produce certain dynamic qualities. By becoming aware of these physically through interpreting them in Movement, one may be able to appreciate better the visual impression.

We do not think that by mentioning the above examples we exhaust all of the existing possibilities. We feel that much benefit could be derived from co-operation with experts from other areas towards further developing the ideas we have presented and so establishing more integrated methods of teaching.

7 Some Psychological Aspects of Movement

All animals need Movement for survival—they search for food, for a mate, they patrol and guard their territory and they play. Man is no exception to this, for he too needs Movement for similar reasons; although in western society opportunities for Movement seem to decrease as people become more affluent and can afford to provide themselves with mechanical aids.

From a very early age man expresses his movement needs clearly— initially through exploration and investigation related to Body Awareness. Babies feel with their fingers and mouths and manipulate joints into a great variety of positions, discovering and "feeling" Movement of each part of their bodies. At a later stage of development they learn to feel the strength of muscles as they first crawl and then walk. Consistent exploration of *what* they can move, *how* they can move and *where* these movements can take them takes place. As children explore these possibilities of Movement they are developing the kinesthetic sense—the "feeling" for Movement concerned not only with movement of muscles but with muscular responses to a number of stimuli from the senses of balance, sight and touch. An integration of all these is important in keeping the body balanced and oriented in Space as well as in playing a part in the formation of a correct body image. With further development the kinesthetic sense takes on a decisive role in how children function and react to the different situations facing them in growing up. In education, for example, psychologists see the need for normal development of these gross motor skills and state that they have a considerable influence on a child's ability to read, write and perform other conceptual skills.

70

During the growing up process children develop certain movement patterns, some copied from their peers or their elders and others which they develop for themselves. These become integrated and form the style of Movement of an individual. The different styles or ways of moving can easily be observed in any situation in which Movement, in any form, plays a part. As teachers we are aware of this and often quite unconsciously assess students by their movement reactions in certain situations, e.g., a student's posture may stiffen slightly if he feels annoyed or threatened, he may flop and sit in an open position if he feels relaxed and secure; small gestures of the hand (twiddling of fingers), legs, face or head can be an indication of tension or boredom. Frequently these small movements—referred to by psychologists as accessory movements—are quite unconscious and are then a reflection of a person's inner attitudes, feelings and emotion. Larger or more conscious movements, viz., walking, contain a large number of acquired mannerisms and bear little relationship to what a person actually thinks or feels. A firm and determined walk, for example, may be a mannerism used to cover up self-consciousness, and an all too quiet stance may hide anger or agitation. What initially was a conscious control over emotions and unreleased feelings may build up tension and anxieties to such an extent that postural defects—such as a stoop from always drawing into oneself or a rigid posture from constantly holding back anger—may result.

As already stated, any movement can be analysed as to the amount of Space it takes up, the degree of Force used, its Rhythm and the amount of Time it takes to complete it. By observation of the movement behaviour of any person certain patterns and attitudes towards each of these aspects can be noted. These observations, if conducted over a period of time and interpreted as to what they mean in terms of feeling, can give an assessment of the person's basic inner attitude. For example, it can be seen that a person uses a great deal of Space, that his natural attitude to Force is light and that he moves slowly from point to point, which perhaps reflects the inner attitude of a "dreamer". A person with these particular attitudes may become very tense if he is required to perform actions diametrically opposed to those which he would normally use. This sometimes can be observed in the classroom situation when a naturally slow person, faced with the fast work required for examinations, breaks down.

In Creative Movement, where students are involved with movement tasks, their affinities to certain types of movements will become apparent and reflect some of their inner attitudes. In exploring all the qualities of Movement, a student is able to experience also those which are foreign to him. By doing this in a controlled situation, the student will allow himself to express latent or less prominent feelings in Movement, and this may enable him to adapt himself more readily to tensions and problems which he encounters. (It is of interest to note here that in our work with psychiatric patients, remarks were made regarding the difficulty of concealing thoughts

71

and feelings in movement therapy; in group sessions, which are conducted on a verbal level, little difficulty in hiding feelings is seen.)

When working creatively with Movement, students combine and integrate their physical, emotional and intellectual abilities and are able to communicate their ideas at a non-verbal level. For some students who have difficulties in expressing themselves verbally, Creative Movement can be seen as a way of giving them more confidence in themselves and this should eventually carry over into other situations.

In many countries the contribution that Movement makes to education as a whole has been overlooked. In this book we have endeavoured to draw attention to the important role that it can play in combining creative abilities and physical skills. Creative Movement, by its very nature, demands complete involvement of all faculties and provides a valuable learning situation. Teachers who have learned to observe Movement, both in everyday activities and in the Creative Movement lesson, are bound to gain a greater understanding of their students as well as perhaps of themselves.

Bibliography

Bruce, Valerie. *Dance and Dance Drama in Education*. Pergamon Press Ltd., London, 1965.

Bruner, Jerome S. *The Process of Education*. Harvard University Press, Cambridge, Massachusetts, 1965.

Canner, Norma & Klebanoff, Harriett. *. . . and a Time to Dance*. Beacon Press, Boston, 1968.

Hawkins, Alma M. *Creating through Dance*. Prentice Hall, Englewood Cliffs, New Jersey, 1969.

H'Doubler, Margaret N. *Dance, A Creative Art Experience*. 2nd Ed. University of Wisconsin Press, Madison, Milwaukee, and London, 1966.

Hughes, Langston. *The First Book of Rhythms*. Edmund Ward, London, 1964.

Humphrey, Doris. *The Art of Making Dances*. Grove Press Inc., New York, 1959.

Kirstein, Lincoln. *Dance, A Short History of Classic Theatrical Dancing*. 3rd Ed. Dance Horizon Inc., New York, 1969.

Kraus, Richard. *History of Dance in Art and Education*. Prentice Hall, Englewood Cliffs, New Jersey, 1969.

Laban, Rudolf. *The Mastery of Movement*. 2nd Ed. Macdonald & Evans, London, 1960.

Laban, Rudolf. *Modern Educational Dance*. 2nd Ed. Macdonald & Evans, London, 1963.

Laban, Rudolf & Lawrence, F. C. *Effort*. Macdonald & Evans, London, 1963.

Lamb, Warren. *Posture and Gesture*. G. Duckworth & Co. Ltd., London, 1965.

Lockhart, Aileene. *Modern Dance, Building and Teaching Lessons*. Wm. C. Brown Company Publ., Dubuque, Iowa, 1966.

Martin, John. *Introduction to the Dance*. Dance Horizon Inc., New York, 1968.

Mettler, Barbara. *Materials of Dance as a Creative Art Activity*. Mettler Studios, Tucson, Arizona, 1960.

Mettler, Barbara. *Nine Articles on Dance*. Mettler Studios, Boston, Mass.

North, Marion. *A Simple Guide to Movement Teaching*. 4th Ed., Marion North, London, 1964.

Preston, Valerie. *A Handbook of Modern Educational Dance*. Macdonald & Evans, London, 1963.

Rowen, Betty. *Learning through Movement*. Teachers College Press, Columbia University, New York, 1963.

Russell, Joan. *Creative Dance in the Primary School*. Macdonald & Evans, London, 1965.

Stagner, Ross & Karwoski, T. F. *Psychology*. McGraw-Hill Book Company, Inc., New York, 1952.

Telford, Charles W. & Sawrey, James M. *Psychology*. Brooks/Cole Publish. . Co., Belmont, Calif., 1968.

The Ministry of Education and the Central Office of Information. *Moving and Growing*. Her Majesty's Stationery Office, London, 1952.